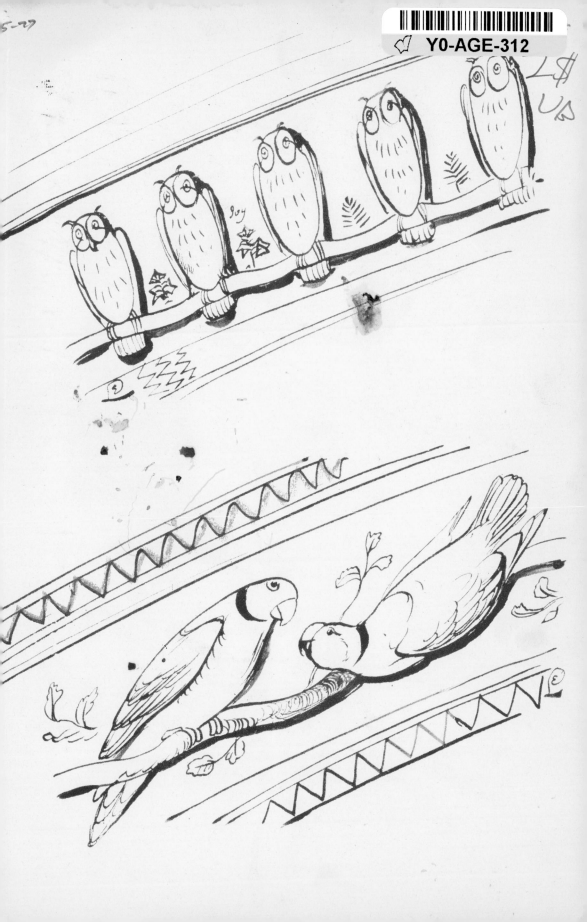

TEAPOTS AND QUAILS

TEAPOTS
AND
QUAILS

And Other New Nonsenses

by

EDWARD LEAR

*

Edited and Introduced by
ANGUS DAVIDSON AND PHILIP HOFER

*

LONDON
JOHN MURRAY ALBEMARLE STREET

All the material in this book is hitherto unpublished
except for a few of the Limericks which were published
in 1933 by the late William B. Osgood Field in *Edward
Lear on my Shelves*, privately printed and limited to one
hundred and fifty-five numbered and signed copies.

First Edition . . November 1953
Reprinted . . . . January 1954

Printed in Great Britain by Bradford & Dickens, London, W.C.1,
and published by John Murray (Publishers) Ltd.
and Harvard University Press
Ltd

CONTENTS

INTRODUCTION BY ANGUS
DAVIDSON *Page 7*

*

FOREWORD BY PHILIP HOFER
Page 11

*

TEAPOTS AND QUAILS SEQUENCE
Page 15

*

LIMERICKS *Page 44*

*

THE ADVENTURES OF MR. LEAR,
THE POLLY AND THE PUSSEYBITE
Page 50

*

FLORA NONSENSICA *Page 56*

*

THE SCROOBIOUS PIP *Page 60*

*

COLD ARE THE CRABS *Page 63*

Apl. 21. 1849.

Introduction

*

LEAR used to say, in later life, that he could remember being taken out of bed, wrapped in a blanket, and held at an upper window of the big house at Highgate where he was born—which looked, from the top of its steep hill, far out over London—to watch the fireworks that celebrated the victory of Waterloo. He was three years old at the time : he was, in fact, born in May 1812, the youngest of an enormous family which, after the bankruptcy and ruin of the father, dispersed to the four winds. The delicate, short-sighted little boy was brought up by his eldest sister Ann, twenty-one years older than himself, and at fifteen was already beginning to earn his living by doing commissioned drawings, of medical and other subjects, for a few shillings. With diligence he perfected his technique as a natural history draughtsman, and this led to his being employed by the Zoological Society to make drawings of the parrots at the Zoo, to other commissions from distinguished naturalists, and finally (when he was still no more than twenty) to an invitation from Lord Derby to stay for a long period at Knowsley Hall near Liverpool and make drawings of the birds and animals in his private " menagerie " there. Lear's natural history drawings show a precise scientific knowledge and observation, an exquisite skill in the delineation of minute and accurate detail, and also the deeper perception and constructive sense of an artist. But his eyesight, always weak, prevented his continuing in this very exacting type of work, and he decided to take to landscape instead: he made up his mind to become a " topographical landscape painter."

The decision brought with it two great advantages. It would allow him, with his restless, inquisitive nature, to achieve one of his greatest ambitions— to travel; and it would give him a perennial pretext for avoiding the English winter, to the benefit of the bronchitis and asthma to which he was prone. And so a traveller he became, a traveller for the rest of his life, in many different lands. He visited India and Ceylon, Egypt and Arabia and Asia Minor, Syria and Palestine. Italy he explored from end to end; his first travel books were written about it; his last years were spent at San Remo, and there, in 1888, he died. But it was Greece that remained, all his life, the country that he loved best; its " divinest beauty," he wrote, charmed him from the moment of his first visit. He traversed the whole of the Greek Peninsula, in journeys that were long, laborious, and extremely uncomfortable, visiting not only the ruins of classical magnificence but the wild and barbarous mountain regions, the monasteries of Mount Athos, the unfrequented fastnesses of Albania; often in danger, often ill, he worked indefatigably. Later he set up his headquarters in Corfu and from there made more expeditions to the Greek mainland and to the other islands of the Ionian Sea. It is amongst the harvest of work that he brought back from these journeys that some of his finest water-colours are to be found.

For Lear, as a water-colourist, has achieved a measure of fame which he himself never expected—a fame far exceeded, however, by his fame in another field much more remote from his strictly professional activities, that of his nonsense writings. Professionally, he considered himself as a painter of large landscapes in oils; yet it was precisely here that his genuine artistic talent found least scope. His enormous oils are truly " topographical landscapes," little more than formal, accurate illustrations of well-chosen views, stiff, detailed, lifeless. In the water-colours, on the other hand, he was creating, not copying; in these, painted for his own pleasure or as studies for his larger works, he could be wholly himself; in these he evolved a personal style which gave him complete liberty to express spontaneously the feeling of a true artist, undistracted by superfluous detail, unfettered by the Pre-Raphaelite influence which admiration for his friend Holman Hunt had superimposed upon his oil painting. Draughtsmanship was always his main concern, and in the water-colours his line is supple, sweeping, expressive. His sense of space, his feeling for the " bones " of a landscape and for the sculptural forms of mountains, are entirely individual. His colour too is delicate and subtle, playing an essential though secondary part in the complete design. These water-colour landscapes are worthy descendants of the great English tradition of Turner, Girtin and De Wint.

The period of almost four years that he spent at Knowsley was of inestimable and far-reaching importance in Lear's life. Not only was he introduced into an exalted social circle, in which he formed many lasting friendships, and in which the future landscape-painter secured many future patrons; not only did he profit by a study of the pictures, particularly the fine collection of the English water-colourists, in Lord Derby's galleries; not only were the results of his labours in the " menagerie," later to be published in book form, highly esteemed: but those four years saw also the beginnings of another and a very different book, a book that was to bring him a fame and an immortality that all his drawings of birds and animals could never have given him—the *Book of Nonsense*.

Amongst the inhabitants, permanent or transitory, of Knowsley, were a number of children, Lord Derby's grandchildren and great-nephews and

great-nieces; and when, as quite often happened, the young Lear, himself
of a buoyant and cheerful disposition, found the distinguished social atmosphere
of the house-party a little heavy, a little dull, he would take refuge in the
nurseries, where he was always certain of a welcome and where his jokes and
funny drawings found instant and uproarious appreciation. For Lear was one
of those rare beings who are able, instinctively, to understand and feel at ease
with children; and children, consequently, were at ease with him. " I remem-
ber perfectly," wrote one who, as a child, had known him, " the towering,
bearded, spectacled man . . . talking in a way which made one feel at once
that he was ' all right ' . . . I cannot remember a single word of what he said.
There only remains a general, but very strong, pervading sense of well-being
and innate rectitude from the standpoint of eight years old. I knew he was
' safe ' . . ." It was this ability to enter into the minds of children that
inspired Lear to compose what he called his " nonsenses "; and indeed he
himself remained, all his life, something of a child.

And so the first *Book of Nonsense* was born. Lear collected the limericks
he had invented for the children at Knowsley, added others he had written
and illustrated later, for other children, and the book appeared in 1846.
His name was not mentioned: the author was to be known merely as " Derry
down Derry." The book had an immediate, though modest, success—of so
limited a kind, however, that no second edition was called for till ten years
later. After that its reputation spread more and more widely: it ran into
nearly thirty editions even in Lear's own lifetime, and became known,
finally, wherever the English language is spoken. It was soon followed by
other nonsense works, and Lear found himself growing famous—though not
quite in the manner he had intended. Yet one or two of his friends recorded
their opinion that, in his heart of hearts, he was more proud of his nonsense
poems than of his paintings: and certainly in later life, when ill-health and
loneliness brought with them frequent and terrible fits of depression, they
became of increasing importance to him as a vehicle of his deepest feelings.
Poems such as *The Yonghy-Bonghy-Bo*, *The Dong with the Luminous Nose* and
Incidents in the Life of my Uncle Arly, though they are pure " nonsense," show
not only a profound sense of rhythm and of the musical sound of words, but
hold an echo of deep melancholy and an emotional force that, deriving from
life itself, transcends its means of expression and acquires a genuinely moving
quality.

Lear was the " Adopty Duncle " of countless children—children of
friends in whose houses he stayed, children of strangers whom he met by
chance on his travels, in trains or hotels; and it was to these children—almost
as much for his own pleasure, one suspects, as for theirs—that the nonsense

rhymes and drawings were given. Small wonder that many of them have not survived intact. *The Adventures of Mr. Lear, the Polly and the Pusseybite*, for instance—now published for the first time, and made, according to Lear's diary, "for Emma Parkyns's children in 1866"—have suffered, most unfortunately, the loss of two pages. But in many cases, especially with the longer poems, Lear kept copies; or made copies and kept his own drafts. Where the drafts are incomplete, it is probable that no copies had been made; in the case, therefore, of *The Scroobious Pip* and *Cold are the Crabs*, neither of which is complete (though the former is very nearly so) it is unlikely that he ever made copies or ever presented them to children. *Cold are the Crabs*, in any case, is scarcely a poem for children. In this fragment—intended, possibly, to be worked out as a sonnet—we see Lear amusing himself with the creation of a perfectly *serious* poem in the Lear manner, a poem which has strange and romantic echoes of some of his contemporaries—Tennyson ? FitzGerald's *Rubaiyat* ? Matthew Arnold ?—a poem which, having no " story " and not even being " funny," is one of the purest pieces of nonsense he ever wrote.

ANGUS DAVIDSON.

*

Thanks are due to Mr. Franklin Henry Lushington, Lear's literary representative, for permission to publish these hitherto unpublished works: also to the Harvard College Library for the loan of the manuscripts, and to Mr. Philip Hofer, the Harvard Press and Mr. T. J. Wilson for their co-operation in publishing.

Foreword

*

TO American eyes, Edward Lear is a classic example of the impecunious artist who sought fame in a medium above his talents only to find it in an unexpected quarter. Modest to the point of continual embarrassment, he was, nevertheless, like William Blake, possessed of an inner determination to go his own way. Huge oil paintings, and many thousands of Mediterranean and East Indian landscapes in water-colour are the silent witnesses of his persistence and of his industry. But it is not through them primarily that he enjoys his present repute in the United States, although his water-colours are increasingly finding admirers because of their uncanny ability to indicate topographical features, even geological formations, despite a somewhat mannered shorthand. It is, of course, through his inimitable nonsense drawings—in shorthand, too, with the unspoiled, unconscious simplicity of a small child—that he is known. Far less widely, but no less surely, his remarkable scientific drawings of birds and other animals are also acclaimed.

These minor talents, if such they be, are so exceptional that we must examine them in greater detail, leaving his other book illustrations, as in travel diaries of Italy, Corsica, and Greece, and even the illustrations for Tennyson's *Poems* on which he laboured so long, to a period more in tune with their spirit. Lear's ornithological drawings suit our present taste. Just recently they have been rediscovered in England by Brian Reade in an article in *Signature* (1947) which he later developed into a monograph where Lear's *Parrots* (1830-2) are reproduced (Duckworth, 1949) on a reduced scale. There he rightly says that the best of Lear's bird lithographs, made early in his career, before ill health and none too strong eyesight forced him to discontinue such minutely detailed work, are of a very high order. Even Audubon is sometimes hardly more impressive. He is scarcely ever so accurate. But the books in which Lear's birds (and other animals) occur are now scarce and expensive. They will never be properly known unless more popular editions, like the one on the parrots, appear. One of the best is also Lear's last work in this area: the *Knowsley Menagerie*, privately published by the Earl of Derby in 1846.

Early success in so difficult a field encouraged Lear. One might call 1846 the most notable date in his career as an artist in the public eye. For in that year Queen Victoria also engaged him to give her twelve drawing lessons, and Lear's first *Book of Nonsense* was published. He had drifted, almost unconsciously, into this region of his special genius. Here he was an innovator, and a figure almost without parallel for many years. Perhaps because we now value witty caricature and primitive art in protest against the frustration and complexity of our times, we may over-value Lear's nonsense drawings today. But this seems unlikely. Rather, we may increasingly acclaim him a pioneer in simplified sophistication; a witty, perhaps unconscious, inspirer of artistic "double talk." If so, he is important, for these qualities promise to remain a feature of our newspaper, magazine, and poster art for many years to come.

Other writers have already drawn attention to the affinity between James Thurber's drawings for *The New Yorker* and the nonsense drawings of Edward Lear. This relationship can be perceived in many subjects in this book. Yet although the analogies are striking, there is no reason to suppose that they were consciously achieved. At numerous periods in art history, often far apart, artists have had the same ideas, and have then expressed them similarly without the slightest reference to each other. The importance of either Lear or Thurber does not primarily depend upon originality, but upon the appeal of both to all ages and conditions of man.

Lear directed his nonsense drawings, like his verses and limericks, from the start at children. He shared their sense of the ridiculous and pleasure at coupling incongruous things. But it was no time before his contemporaries fell under the spell of Lear's charm. The *Book of Nonsense*, and other nonsense titles which followed, were a result of wide cumulative demand, even though certain of their special qualities and overtones were not appreciated till our day. Had they been, we would probably not have been able to offer so many hitherto unpublished drawings so long after Lear died. Behind a quick and simple draughtsmanship we detect a keen eye for the variety of nature, and a brilliant emphasis on essential detail. These nonsense drawings are the very antithesis of the parrot drawings, and of most of the topographical scenes. But only long training in the former—indeed in every kind of drawing—gave Lear the ability, as it did Rembrandt, to express himself also in the simplest terms. No novice should try to emulate Lear unless he is gifted by the gods.

PHILIP HOFER.

*

The original drawings and manuscripts, from which the reproductions in this book were made, most recently belonged either to William B. Osgood Field of New York, who had much the larger proportion, or to the writer of this foreword. In 1942, by common consent, both placed their "Leariana" in the Harvard College Library so that the various phases of Lear's graphic work and writing might be studied in one collection. Some of the finest items were willed to Sir Franklin Lushington, the artist's intimate friend and executor. These were sold at Sotheby's, in London, by order of Sir Franklin's daughter on March 27, 1929. Another important group, consisting particularly of drawings, belonged to Lord Northbrook, who invited Lear to India in 1873-4. They were also sold at Sotheby's a few months later (November 27, 1929). Thus the nucleus of the present Harvard collection was formed which is the most extensive in the United States, although some fine manuscripts, drawings, and books are owned by private collectors, notably in New York, Maryland, Chicago, Cambridge, and Washington.

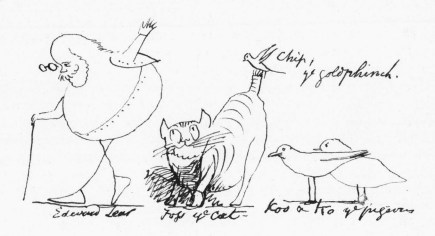

Teapots and Quails,
Snuffers and snails,
Set him a sailing
and see how he sails!

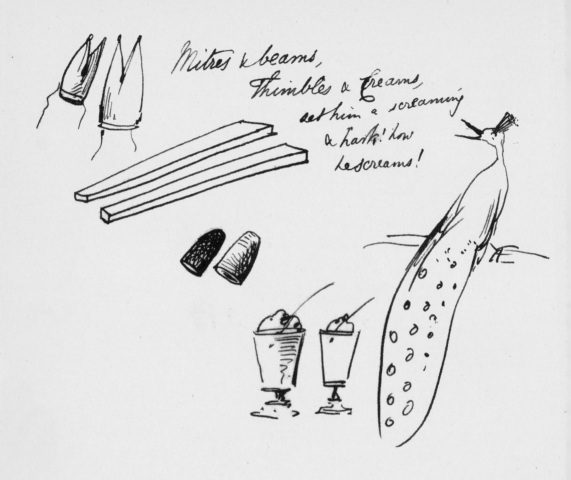

Mitres and beams,
Thimbles and Creams,
Set him a screaming
and hark! how he screams!

Houses and Kings,
Whiskers and Swings,
Set him a stinging
and see how he stings!

Ribands & pigs,
Helmets & Figs, set him a jigging
& see how he jigs.

Ribands and Pigs,
Helmets and Figs,
Set him a jigging
and see how he jigs!

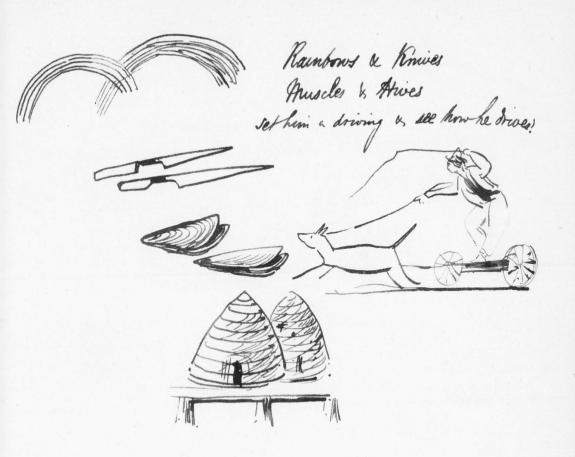

Rainbows and Knives,
Muscles and Hives,
Set him a driving
and see how he drives!

Tadpoles & Tops,
Teacups & Mops,
set him a hopping & see how he hops!

Tadpoles and Tops,
Teacups and Mops,
Set him a hopping
and see how he hops!

Herons and Sweeps,
Turbans and Sheeps,

Herons and Sweeps,
Turbans and Sheeps,
Set him a weeping
and see how he weeps!

Lobsters & owls,
Scissors and fowls,
Set him a howling
& hark how he howls! —

Lobsters and owls,
Scissors and fowls,
Set him a howling
and hark how he howls!

Eagles and pears,
Slippers and Bears,
Set him a staring
and see how he stares!

Sofas and bees,
Camels and Keys,
Set him a sneezing
and see how he'll sneeze!

Wafers and Bears,
Ladders and Squares,
Set him a staring
and see how he stares!

Cutlets and eyes,
Swallows and pies,
Set it a flying
and see how it flies!

Thistles and Moles,
Crumpets and Soles,
Set it a rolling
and see how it rolls!

Tea urns and Pews,
Muscles and Jews,
Set him a mewing
and hear how he mews!

Watches and Oaks,
Custards and Cloaks,
Set him a poking
and see how he pokes!

Bonnets and Legs,
Steamboats and Eggs,
Set him a begging
and see how he begs!

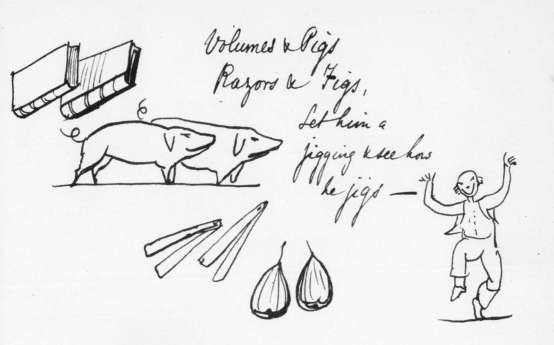

Volumes and Pigs,
Razors and Figs,
Set him a jigging
and see how he jigs!

Hurdles and Mumps,
Poodles and pumps,
Set it a jumping
and see how he jumps!

Pancakes and Fins,
Roses and Pins,
Set him a grinning
and see how he grins!

Gruel and prawns,
Bracelets and Thorns,
Set him a yawning
and see how he yawns!

chimnies & Wings,
Sailors & Rings,
set him a singing
& hark how he sings!

Chimnies and Wings,
Sailors and Rings,
Set him a singing
and hark how he sings!

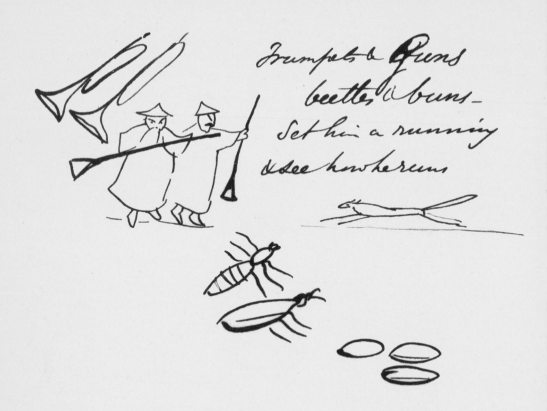

Trumpets and Guns,
beetles and buns,
Set him a running
and see how he runs!

Saucers & tops,
Lobsters & Mops,
Set it a hopping, & see how he hops!

Saucers and tops,
Lobsters and Mops,
Set it a hopping
and see how he hops!

Puddings and beams,
Cobwebs and creams,
Set him a screaming
and hear how he screams!

Rainbows and Wives,
Puppies and Hives,
Set him a driving
and see how he drives!

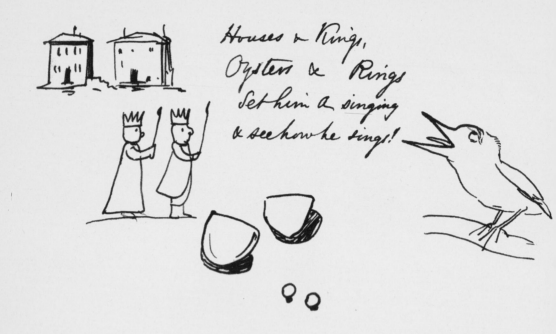

Houses and Kings,
Oysters and Rings,
Set him a singing
and see how he sings!

Scissars & Fowls,
Filberd & Owls
Set him a howling
& see how he
howls —

Scissors and Fowls,
Filberts and Owls,
Set him a howling
and see how he howls!

Blackbirds and ferns,
Spiders and Churns,
Set it a turning
and see how it turns!

LIMERICKS

There was an old person of Diss,
Who said, " It is this! It is this! "
When they said " What? or which? "—He jumped into a ditch,
  Which absorbed that old person of Diss.

There was an old person of Harrow
Who bought a mahogany barrow,
For he said to his wife, " You're the joy of my life!
  " And I'll wheel you all day in this barrow! "

There was an old person of Twickenham,
Who whipped his four horses to quicken 'em;
When they stood on one leg, He said faintly, " I beg
       "We may go back directly to Twickenham!"

There was an old person of Brussels,
Who lived upon Brandy and Mussels.
When he rushed through the town, He knocked most people down,
       Which distressed all the people of Brussels.

There was an old person of Cheam,
Who said, " It is just like a dream,
" When I play on the drum, and wear rings on my thumb
"In the beautiful meadows of Cheam!"

There was an old man of Carlisle,
Who was left on a desolate isle:
Where he fed upon cakes, and lived wholly with snakes,
Who danced with that man of Carlisle.

There was an old man of the hills,
Who lived upon Syrup of Squills;
Which he drank all night long, To the sound of a gong,
    That persistent old man of the hills.

There was an old person of Bradley
Who sang all so loudly and sadly;
With a poker and tongs, He beat time to his songs,
    That melodious old person of Bradley!

There was an old man of Girgenti,
Who lived in profusion and plenty;
He lay on two chairs, and ate thousands of pears,
    That susceptible man of Girgenti.

There was a young man in Iowa
Who exclaimed, "Where on earth shall I stow her!"
Of his sister he spoke, who was felled by an Oak
    Which abound in the plains of Iowa.

THE ADVENTURES OF MR. LEAR, THE POLLY AND THE PUSSEYBITE

Of this manuscript two pages, each presumably containing two drawings, are missing.

d

THE ADVENTURES OF MR. LEAR, THE POLLY AND THE PUSSEYBITE
ON THEIR WAY TO THE RITERTITLE MOUNTAINS

Aug. 23. 1866.
1, Upper Hyde Park Gardens.

*

Mr. Lear goes out a walking with a Polly and the Pusseybite.

Mr. Lear, feeling tired, and also the Polly and the Pusseybite, sit down on a wall to rest.

Mr. Lear, the Polly and the Pusseybite go into a shop to buy a Numbrella, because it began to rain.

Mr. Lear, the Polly and the Pusseybite having purchased umbrellas, proceed on their walk.

Mr. Lear, the Polly and the Pusseybite arrive at a bridge, which being broken they do not know what to do.

Mr. Lear, the Polly and the Pusseybite all tumble promiscuous into the raging river and become quite wet.

A page missing here from the manuscript.

Mr. Lear and the Polly and the Pusseybite pursue their journey in a benevolent boat.

Mr. Lear and the Polly and the Pusseybite incidentally fall over an unexpected cataract, and are all dashed to atoms.

A page missing here from the manuscript.

The 2 venerable Jebusites fasten the remains of Mr. Lear, the Polly and the Pusseybite together, but fail to reconstruct them perfectly as 3 individuals.

Mr. Lear and the Pusseybite and the Pollycat and the 2 Jebusites and the Jerusalem Artichokes and the Octagonal Oysterclippers all tumble into a deep hole and are never seen or distinguished or heard of never more afterwards.

FLORA NONSENSICA

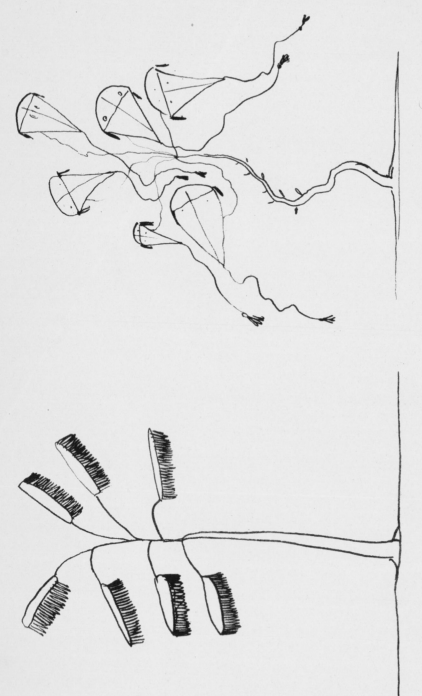

The Kite Tree is a fearful and astonishing vegetable when all the Kites are agitated by a tremendous wind, and endeavour to escape from their strings. The tree does not appear to be of any particular use to society, but would be frequented by small boys if they knew where it grew.

The Clothes-Brush Tree. This most useful natural production does not produce many clothesbrushes, which accounts for those objects being expensive. The omsquombious nature of this extraordinary vegetable it is of course unnecessary to be diffuse upon.

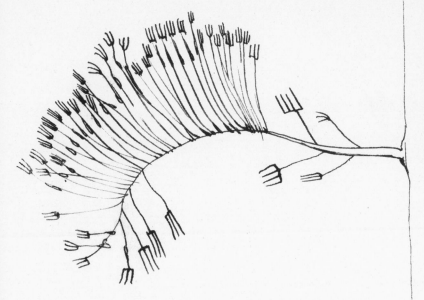

The Fork Tree. This pleasing and amazing Tree never grows above four hundred and sixty three feet in height; nor has any specimen hitherto produced above forty thousand silver forks at one time. If violently shaken it is most probable that many forks would fall off, and in a high wind it is highly possible that all the forks would rattle dreadfully, and produce a musical tinkling to the ears of the happy beholder.

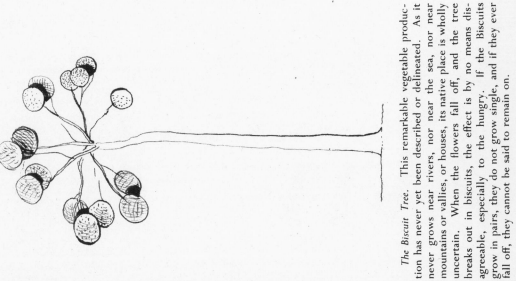

The Biscuit Tree. This remarkable vegetable production has never yet been described or delineated. As it never grows near rivers, nor near the sea, nor near mountains or vallies, or houses, its native place is wholly uncertain. When the flowers fall off, and the tree breaks out in biscuits, the effect is by no means disagreeable, especially to the hungry. If the Biscuits grow in pairs, they do not grow single, and if they ever fall off, they cannot be said to remain on.

The Rabbit Tree

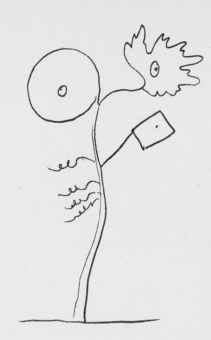

The Clomjombimbilious Tree

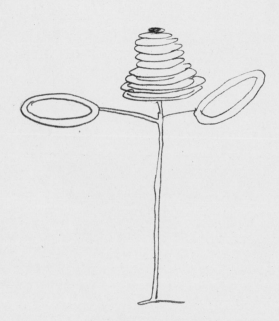

The Dish Tree

Ourbeerdsia Socherishdah

Cheenyoneena Falsaria

The Scroobious Pip

*

The Scroobious Pip went out one day
When the grass was green, and the sky was grey.
Then all the beasts in the world came round
When the Scroobious Pip sat down on the ground.
     The cat and the dog and the kangaroo
     The sheep and the cow and the guineapig too—
     The wolf he howled, the horse he neighed
     The little pig squeaked and the donkey brayed,
     And when the lion began to roar
     There never was heard such a noise before.
     And every beast he stood on the tip
     Of his toes to look at the Scroobious Pip.
At last they said to the Fox—" By far,
You're the wisest beast! You know you are!
Go close to the Scroobious Pip and say,
Tell us all about yourself we pray—
For as yet we can't make out in the least
If you're Fish or Insect, or Bird or Beast."
The Scroobious Pip looked vaguely round
And sang these words with a rumbling sound—
     Chippetty Flip; Flippetty Chip;—
My only name is the Scroobious Pip.

2

The Scroobious Pip from the top of a tree
Saw the distant Jellybolee,—
And all the birds in the world came there,
Flying in crowds all through the air.

      The Vulture and Eagle, the cock and the hen
      The Ostrich the Turkey the Snipe and the Wren;
      The Parrot chattered, the Blackbird sung
      And the owl looked wise but held his tongue,
      And when the Peacock began to scream
      The hullabaloo was quite extreme.
      And every bird he fluttered the tip
      Of his wing as he stared at the Scroobious Pip.
At last they said to the owl—" By far,
You're the wisest Bird—you know you are!
Fly close to the Scroobious Pip and say,
Explain all about yourself we pray—
For as yet we have neither seen nor heard
If you're fish or insect, beast or bird! "
The Scroobious Pip looked gaily round
And sang these words with a chirpy sound—
      Flippetty chip—Chippetty flip—
My only name is the Scroobious Pip.

The Scroobious Pip went into the sea
By the beautiful shore of the Jellybolee—
All the Fish in the world swam round
With a splashing squashy spluttering sound.

      The sprat, the herring, the turbot too
      The shark the sole and the mackerel blue,
      The flounder sputtered, the porpoise puffed

      .   .   .   .

      And when the whale began to spout

      .   .   .   .

      And every fish he shook the tip
      Of his tail as he gazed on the Scroobious Pip.
At last they said to the whale—"By far
You're the biggest Fish—you know you are!
Swim close to the Scroobious Pip and say—
Tell us all about yourself we pray!—
For to know you yourself is our only wish;
Are you beast or insect, bird or fish?"
The Scroobious Pip looked softly round
And sung these words with a liquid sound—
      Pliffity flip, Pliffity flip—
My only name is the Scroobious Pip.

The Scroobious Pip sat under a tree
By the silent shores of the Jellybolee;
All the insects in all the world
About the Scroobious Pip entwirled.
    Beetles and with purple eyes
    Gnats and buzztilential flies—
    Grasshoppers, butterflies, spiders too,
    Wasps and bees and dragon-flies blue,
    And when the gnats began to hum
      bounced like a dismal drum,
    And every insect curled the tip
    Of his snout, and looked at the Scroobious Pip.
At last they said to the Ant—"By far
You're the wisest insect, you know you are!
Creep close to the Scroobious Pip and say—
Tell us all about yourself we pray,
For we can't find out, and we can't tell why—
If you're beast or fish or a bird or a fly."
The Scroobious Pip turned quickly round
And sang these words with a whistly sound
    Wizzeby wip—wizzeby wip—
My only name is the Scroobious Pip.

5

Then all the beasts that walk on the ground
Danced in a circle round and round—
And all the birds that fly in the air
Flew round and round in a circle there,
And all the fish in the Jellybolee
Swum in a circle about the sea,
And all the insects that creep or go
Buzzed in a circle to and fro.
And they roared and sang and whistled and cried
Till the noise was heard from side to side—
    Chippetty tip! Chippetty tip!
It's only name is the Scroobious Pip.

*

Cold are the Crabs

*

Cold are the crabs that crawl on yonder hills,
Colder the cucumbers that grow beneath,
And colder still the brazen chops that wreathe
    The tedious gloom of philosophic pills!
For when the tardy film of nectar fills
The ample bowls of demons and of men,
There lurks the feeble mouse, the homely hen,
    And there the porcupine with all her quills.
Yet much remains—to weave a solemn strain
That lingering sadly—slowly dies away,
Daily departing with departing day.
A pea green gamut on a distant plain
When wily walrusses in congress meet—
    Such such is life—

*

Garden of
Tulips

Byrd

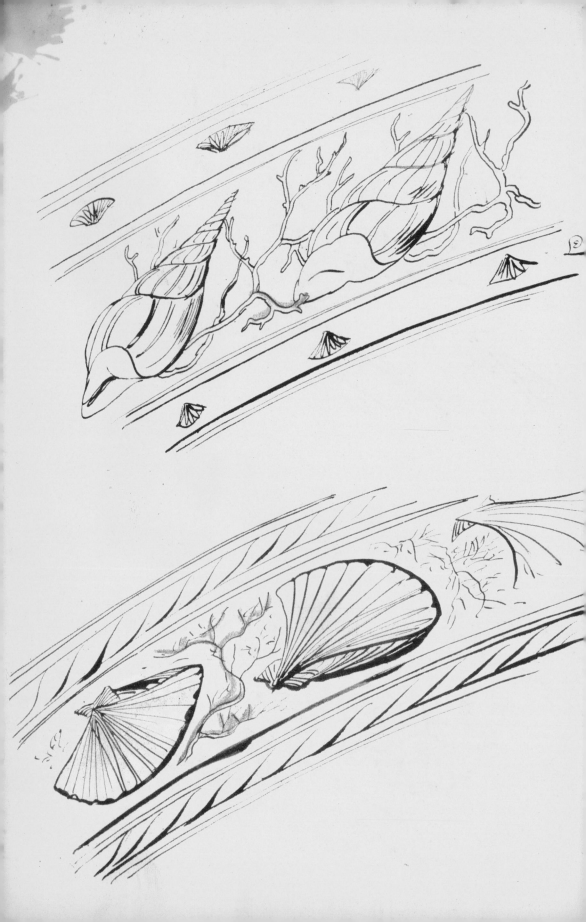